Dialogues with Leo Baeck

Dialogues with Leo Baeck

Translated from German
By Robert Rhée and David Dowdey

iUniverse, Inc.
New York Lincoln Shanghai

Dialogues with Leo Baeck

iUniverse books may be ordered through booksellers or by contacting:

iUniverse
2021 Pine Lake Road, Suite 100
Lincoln, NE 68512
www.iuniverse.com
1-800-Authors (1-800-288-4677)

ISBN-13: 978-0-595-42426-9 (pbk)
ISBN-13: 978-0-595-86761-5 (ebk)
ISBN-10: 0-595-42426-0 (pbk)
ISBN-10: 0-595-86761-8 (ebk)

Printed in the United States of America

This play has been performed on over seventy stages in eleven countries and has won an award from the Leo Baeck Institute. It was first performed in the U.S. at the Malibu Jewish Center to commemorate the 50th anniversary of "Kristallnacht"; the beginning of the major pogroms in Hitler's Germany.

Dr. Leo Baeck, Reform rabbi and foremost religious leader of German Jewry after World War I, acted as its consoler during the Nazi period. Because he was a pacifist, he preached non-resistance.

Rabbi LEO BAECK was born in Germany in 1873, near the Polish border. His community had been strongly influenced by the famous Rabbi Akiba Egar. Here, Baeck acquired the kind of piety and love for God reminiscent of the Jewish mystics of the Middle Ages. Ordained by the liberal seminary in Berlin, he became a quite modern Rabbi. After teaching in Silesia for ten years, he moved to Dusseldorf and from there to Berlin, where he held the post of Rabbi until 1942. During World War I, he served as chaplain with the Kaiser's army on both the Russian and Western front. In 1992, he became President of the German Rabbinical Association in Berlin, was deported to Theresienstadt in 1942, survived and was liberated by the Russians in 1945. He moved to London and taught at the Hebrew Union College. His writings included: "The Essence of Judaism," "This People Israel," and "Judaism and Christianity." In 1948 he visited Los Angeles for the opening of the Leo Baeck Temple. He died in London in 1959.

Our "Dialogue" covered the Period from 1933 to 1945.

◆   ◆   ◆

German author ERWIN SYLVANUS, born in 1917 in Soest, Westphalia (a non-Jew), came from a family of scholars. Like all Germans he was drafted into Hitler's army, but was discharged for health reasons. He is the author of the play "Korczak and his children," the story of sixty-five Jewish orphans from Poland and their orphanage director Dr. Korczak, who accompanied them into the concentration camp. The play (a dialogue) was performed on over seventy stages, in eleven countries, and won Sylvanus an award from the Leo Baeck Institute in 1958. Our play, "Dialogues with Leo Baeck" was first shown on German television in 1966. Sylvanus lived in Germany until his death in 1985.

1

INTRODUCTION

What is the legacy of Rabbi Baeck, as human history is nearing the time of sealing the pages on the twentieth century and opening the pages on the twenty-first century? As we present to the public this play on Baeck's years in Theresienstadt, we realize it is incumbent on us to answer this question. This we will attempt to do.

During Rabbi Baeck's life, in 1948, Rabbi Joshua Liebman offered a portrait of Baeck in his article "A Living Saint: Rabbi Baeck."[1] By then, the war and Baeck's liberation were three years in the past. Baeck was serving as president of the World Union of Progressive Judaism in London. That same year, Baeck visited America on behalf of two famous institutions of liberal Judaism: the Union of American Hebrew Congregations and Hebrew Union College. Just the title of Liebman's article is a hint at the high esteem enjoyed by Baeck this side of the Atlantic.

Leo Baeck's reputation in America as "a saint for our times," as "the Moses of German history,"[2] is based principally on his experiences in Theresienstadt (the thrust of Erwin Sylvanus' Leo Baeck) and on what happened after his liberation. Baeck's life and activities subsequent to the war were in the public eye, not only until his death on 2 November 1956 (reported on 3 November 1956 in The New York Times),[3] but as late as 1965 when Time (19 February) carried an article on Rabbi Baeck. The author states that Baeck "...?is revered as a saint of modern Judaism, and as one of the last towering figures of the German Jewish renaissance that produced such men as Freud, Einstein, Kafka, and Martin Buber.[4] He was, the article also states, "...?one of Germany's great articulators of Reform Judaism."[5]

Adolf Leschnitzer, writing in 1957, in his article "The Unknown Leo Baeck,"[6] maintains that it was only in the last twenty or twenty-five years of his life that Leo Baeck became a public figure. According to Leschnitzer, Baeck failed "...?to win widespread recognition during the first sixty years of his life."[7] Rabbi Kaelter, residing at the time of this writing in Los Angeles and acquainted with Leo Baeck

1

during the pre-war years in Germany, voiced this same opinion.[8] Baeck was, according to Kaelter, not popular but highly respected and admired during the pre-war years. Another Los Angeles resident who knew Baeck, Rabbi Alfred Wolf, remembers life-long traits Baeck never lost, even after he became famous in America: all his life Baeck was weak as a public speaker; he used long sentences and abstract words. Baeck's greatest strength, says Wolf, was as a writer and thinker.[9] Baeck is remembered by Los Angeles Rabbi Bert Woythaler more as a thinker and philosopher than as an organization man or political activist.[10] These men (Kaelter, Wolf, and Woythaler) all remember the modesty and humanity of Baeck: "...?the most modest of all people ... gracious and thankful?..." (Wolf); "...?the most modest person ... truly humble ... In eight years of pulpit preaching Baeck never once used the pronoun 'I'" (Kaelter); ".... a humble person?..." (Woythaler). Heidelberg resident Ruth Ransohoff, a personal acquaintance of this writer and fellow member in a Christian congregation, pays homage to Leo Baeck every year on his birthday, 23 May. Baeck performed her father's, Max Ransohoff's, Bar Mitzvah in Düsseldorf in 1913. Later, both families resided in Berlin. In the Ransohoff home Rabbi Baeck was regarded with the highest esteem and respect.[11]

Notwithstanding his humility, notwithstanding the possibility that he may never have become as famous a figure had the war never started, Baeck was for a few persons "an intellectual hero." Joshua Leibman wrote:

> ... I knew him as one of the foremost scholars in Europe, a master of Greek and Latin, whose published volumes on religion and philosophy were treasured by thinkers everywhere. He was at home not merely on rabbinic literature but in philosophy from Plato through Kant, in the dramas of Shakespeare and Ibsen, in the art of Michelangelo and the music of Beethoven.
>
> Baeck did not, however, dwell in the ivory tower of speculation. He was a great communal leader, serving as the rabbi of the famous Oranienburger Synagogue in Berlin. He was known and respected in the chancelleries and embassies of the German capital as a spokesman of the Jewish people and of human rights. When the Nazis came into power, Rabbi Baeck stood in his distinguished pulpit and preached the living word of God against paganism and the idolatry of the State. These sermons brought him face to face with the Gestapo. As the years passed he was caught in the steel network of the SS men on five different occasions, but so great was the respect accorded this learned Rabbi, by Jew and Christian alike, that the Nazis hesitated to destroy him.[12]

Liebman's article is a continuous accolade and summary of Baeck's later life. Details of the early years are, however, omitted. The article's title, "A Living

Saint: Rabbi Baeck," sets the tone for the reverential stance Liebman maintains throughout the article. Liebman believed that a set of three "almost miraculous" circumstances were responsible for Baeck's survival and ultimate release from the camp at Theresienstadt. First, because the Gestapo has confused two similar names of two rabbis in Berlin, Baeck and Beck, Rabbi Baeck was still living and was sent to Theresienstadt. Second, Liebman believes, was the fact that Baeck's number never occurred in the random drawings of who would be transported to sure death in Auschwitz. In the camp Baeck did bemeaning tasks such as being harnessed to and forced to pull a garbage cart. Behind the Nazi strategy of turning him into a beast of burden "…?there hid the mean hope that the work would break and destroy the man."[13] Upon turning seventy, however, he was released from this duty. He then spent daytime hours visiting sick inmates, bringing comfort and encouragement through his personal faith. To the dying he read from the Pslams—"The Lord is my Shepherd, I shall not want." He testified to his faith that death was the entrance into the world to come, the great rebirth. Baeck also often brought to the hungry bread he had saved up. On 10 November 1988, in a sermon commemorating the fiftieth anniversary of <u>Kristallnacht</u>, Rabbi Wolli Kaelter of Los Angeles recalled a scene in Theresienstadt: "'We have stood at so many gravesides and recited Kaddish and El Male so many times here in Theresienstadt,' said Leo Baeck in 1944 to friends, 'but we have never done anything as a community to celebrate the birth of children. We must plant a tree.' A seedling was smuggled into the camp and planted in a large open place between the walls and the barracks."[14]

Baeck's teachings activities, though strictly forbidden, also filled the nights in the camp. In the darkness crowds huddled together to hear Baeck lecture on philosophy, covering the spectrum from Plato to Kant. He taught children the Hebrew alphabet and told them stories about biblical Patriarchs and Prophets. Ruth Klüger remembers how he taught Bible stories to children in the camp:

> Leo Baeck redete zu uns auf dem Dachboden. Wir saßen zusammengedrängt und hörten den berühmten Berliner Rabbiner. Er erklärte uns, wie man die biblische Geschichte von der Schöpfung müsse, weil die moderne Wissenschaft von Millionen Jahren weiß. Relativität der Zeit. Gottes Tag ist nicht wie unsere Tage und hat nicht etwa nur 24 Stunden…. Ich war ganz bei der Sache, berührt erstens von der festlichen Stimmung, wie wir eng unter den nackten Balken saßen, und zweitens von diesen so schlicht und eindringlich vorgetragenen Ideen. Er gab uns unser Erbe zurück, die Bibel im Geiste der Aufklärung, man konnte besides haben, den alten Mythos, die neue Wissenschaft. Ich war hingerissen, das Leben würde noch schön werden. Baeck muß

ein hochbegabter Prediger gewesen sein—wie würde ich mir sonst das alles gemerkt haben?—dieser treuherzige deutsche Bürger,?...”[15]

A third circumstance, according to Liebman, when Baeck's life was spared, came in April 1945. Eichmann, upon learning of the clerical error that falsely convinced the Gestapo of Baeck's death, had come to announce that Baeck would die the next morning. Having written parting words to his daughter and granddaughter and having retired to await the dawn and the arrival of his executioners, Baeck was greeted at the dawn not by Eichmann but by a Russian soldier with an announcement. He announced the liberation of the camp and the flight of the Nazis. Baeck remained at the camp for another month tending to such grim duties as burying the dead and arranging transportation for the survivors. Not until Baeck delivered a farewell address to the survivors on the text "Be strong and of good courage?..." did he board the military plane and leave.

The concluding part of Liebman's article serves us well in our search for Baeck's legacy. Once again Liebman emphasizes "...?that saintliness is the outstanding characteristic of Leo Baeck."[16] Two of Baeck's most striking qualities Liebman believes, were his profound understanding of the good and evil in human nature, as well as his forgiving attitude. Leonard Baker recounts in his book how Baeck, when offered a chance for vengeance on his persecutors, preferred to wait and leave it in the hands of justice.[17] Furthermore Baeck avoided generalizations or stereotypes that would have damned the whole German nation. He could still recall deeds of kindness performed on behalf of Jews by a Christian German boy and a German countess. Most unusual, considering all that the Jewish people had endured, was the total absence of pessimism or bitterness. He maintained an affirmative outlook and could still be stimulated by new ideas and goals. "Most remarkable," says Liebman, "is that he [Baeck] has totally escaped self-pity."[18] How astonishing that Baeck at this juncture in his life could still say, "God made the earth, but now man must make it a realm of God" or "The true task of man is to create for himself a noble memory, a mind filled with grandeur, forgiveness, restless ideals, and the dynamic ethical ferment preached by all religions at their best."[19]

Liebman's portrait of Baeck, published in June 1948, evidently was thought worth of an even wider audience, since Reader's Digest published a condensed version one month later in July entitled "The most Unforgettable Character I've Met."

In 1953, on the occasion of his turning 80, over three years before Baeck's death in 1956, Time described Baeck as "...?one who is venerated as a hero, a scholar, and a man of God."[20] Whereas Liebman's article focuses on Baeck's saintliness in the context of Theresienstadt and afterwards and does not give many facts of his early life, the <u>Time</u> article points out that he was born in Lissa, Posen (then German territory), the studied in Breslau and Berlin. Baeck's famous <u>Das Wesen des Judentums</u> (1905) is referred to, but the fact is not mentioned that the reason Baeck wrote the book is closely linked to the appearance in 1900 of Adolf von Harnack's <u>Das Wesen des Christentums</u>, in which Judaism is described as spiritually inferior to Christianity. Harnack attempted to deny the roots of Christianity in the Jewish Old Testament. Baeck even dared to uphold the historicity of Christianity and the church in this point. During World War I, Baeck served as a chaplain. As far as most of the world was concerned, the years 1912 through 1933 were years of relative obscurity for Baeck. He settled in Berlin, dividing his professional responsibilities between writing and being the spiritual leader of the Oranienburger street synagogue. During the Berlin years (1918-1939) he taught Midrash and homiletics at the Berliner <u>Hochschule für die Wissenschaft des Judentums</u>. In 1922 he was elected as chairman of the <u>Allgemeinen deutschen Rabbinerverbandes</u>. Beginning in 1925, he became president of B'nai B'rith. He was also on the committee of the <u>Central-Verein deutscher Staatsbürger jüdischen Glaubens</u>. Baeck wrote extensively in this organization's journal, <u>C. V. Zeitung</u>, as well as in its periodical, <u>Der Morgen</u>.[21] The rest of Baeck's life—his election in 1933 to presidency of the <u>Reichsvertretung der Juden in Deutschland</u>, the menacing ascendancy of the Nazis to power, offers to come to America, threats from the Nazis, his arrest, Theresienstadt, the liberation by the Russians, and the post-war years of enjoying high esteem and respect—is more familiar and is mainly what Sylvanus presents in his play.

As we continue to search out Baeck's legacy and to take precaution that the halo does not glow too brightly after Liebman's article, it is helpful to refer back to Leschnitzer's article. For six years, 1933 through 1939, he [Leschnitzer] worked closely with Baeck in the <u>Rechsvertretung</u>, thus was qualified to speak on intimate aspects of Baeck's personality. By no means is the present writer implying that Leschnitzer denigrates Baeck's reputation. Quite the contrary! In the concluding lines he lauds Baeck and maintains that Baeck was less the man who strove for greatness and significance and more the man who strove only for righteousness.[22] What are some of the "unknowns" Leschnitzer discloses about Baeck?

Totally in agreement with what Rabbi Kaelter said in a personal interview[23] that Baeck did not like posing, Leschnitzer also emphasizes that Baeck, first and formost, avoided ostentatious display. Baeck's self-control, whether from effort or whether from upbringing, was only on the surface. At times Baeck's great reserves of energy, passion, and ardor could break forth and dispel his tranquil, serene appearance. In the office of the <u>Reichsvertretung</u> he was known as the "Cardinal" because of his diplomatic, prudent air. He could, however, be severe in his judgments of others. He had high standards not only for himself, but also for others. Leschnitzer says Baeck's judgments were "…?based on keen observation, painstaking appraisal, and instinctively accurate assessment of people."[24] Baeck's powerful metaphors and turns of phrase were, no doubt, writes Leschnitzer, attributable to his humanistic education, being steeped in Greek and Roman authors and combined with a generous portion of Jewish lore. Colleagues in the office of the <u>Reichsvertretung</u> witnessed Baeck's fortitude and personal convictions. Despite threatening, pessimistic news about the Nazi regime, Baeck remained unnerved. For purposes of comparison, Leschnitzer divides great men into two groups. Goethe, aware of his achievements and greatness, represents one group. Bach, not fully aware of his achievements and significance, represents the other group. We are compelled to say that Baeck was of the latter group. Leschnitzer subtly suggests that Baeck belonged to the thirty-six righteous men of his generation who sustained the world. Thus, although Leschnitzer eulogizes Baeck differently from Liebman, in the end he sounds a chord in harmony with Liebman: Baeck's greatness was his saintliness.

In a lecture on 28 January 1958 at the Bremer Volkshochschule, Karl Heinrich Rengstorf indicated how at that time it was not to be taken for granted that one would speak of Leo Baeck: "Von Leo Baeck als geistiger Gestalt unserer Zeit zu sprechen, ist auf deutschem Boden nicht so selbstverständlich, wie es auf den ersten Blick scheinen könnte."[25] He eulogized Baeck as one of the great guardians of the spirit. Even at that time in Germany Rengstorf regrets that just one year after Baeck's death hardly anyone knew who he was when the German postal service published a stamp commemorating him. Rengstorf wants to remind his audience of the urgency of preserving Baeck's memory and legacy. Baeck's early life and education are summariazed in an excellent and compact manner. The history of the little hometown of Baeck, Lissa in Poland, is described by Rengstorf as no other source describes it. Lissa was the third largest Jewish community in Posen, and the fifth largest in Prussia. It was also in Lissa that Amos Comenius (1592–1670), a bishop of the Brethren Church, began a <u>Gymnasium</u> where Baeck himself later studied. At this school Baeck "…?begegnete ganz unmittlebar auch einem Christentum, das seines Reichstums gewiß war, das sich aber nicht zuerst zur Durchsetzung seines Rechtes berufen war wußte, sondern zum Dienst mit dem Ziele, das göttliche Ebenbild im Menschen zur Entfaltun zu bringen."

(p. 8) Rengstorf presents the otherwise well-known facts of Baeck's life and experiences in Theresienstadt. Truly to be admired, says Rengstorf, is Baeck's attitude in the hour of deliverance from the camp. Baeck refused to carry out any vengeance on his tormentors. "Diese Haltung zeigt seine ganz menschliche Größe, wie sie zur edelsten Bewährung unter denkbar menschenunwürdigen Verhältnissen gereift war." (p. 10) In the last part of his eulogy, Rengstorf underscores the extraordinary quality of Baeck's life, the power and magic of his personality. Amidst all the mindlessness and inhumanity of the twentieth century it is Baeck who stands as one of the great representatives of the spirit and of humaneness. Rengstorf concludes by pointing out three important qualities that serve to epitomize what Baeck's life meant. First, Baeck was at once consciously and in a modern sense Jewish. For Baeck, being Jewish was inseparable from his life. Baeck felt himself obligated to face the challenges of being Jewish in the modern world, rather than escaping or assimilating. Second, Baeck was a man of perfected inner freedom. The two characteristics that best showed his were his high personal courage and his almost unlimited personal sense of loyalty. By no means did this mean Baeck was a man of compromise. Within German Jewry he often served as a bridge between feuding parties. Baeck was able to preserve the credibility of German Jewry and its intellectual heritage in the face of the persecutors. He made it possible for German Jewry to have a chance to revive itself after the war. Third, since for Baeck matters of the spirit were not just of human origin, rather of God's origin, humans ceased to be made in the image of God when they renounced the spirit. To renounce the spirit and to renounce God were for Baeck synonymous. Rengstorf believes Baeck's pastoral role throughout his life, especially after the war, cannot be emphasized enough. Baeck's example and his writings on the topic are, according to Rengstorf, instructive for Christians. By mentioning so many positive qualities of Baeck's, Rengstorf runs the risk of appearing to be less than objective. Nonetheless, he was proceeding thusly not in order to hide what was all too human and imperfect about Baeck, but rather to illustrate that "…?Gott größer ist als das Menschenherz und daß sein Geist immer noch seine Diener zu prägen vermag." (pp. 14-15) The succinct portrait of Baeck presented by Rengstorf deserves not to be forgotten in our attempt to trace out the legacy of Leo Baeck.

The legacy of Rabbi Baeck has also been preserved in Rabbi Albert Friedlander's book Leo Baeck. Teacher of Theresienstadt.[26] Friedlander, once a student of Baeck's and by any measure certainly an admirer, is nevertheless more reserved in idolization. For example, he shies away from the term "saintliness." Friedlander says Baeck "…?was not 'the saint of Theresienstadt,' as some would have it. He was a man, with flaws and weaknesses. He made mistakes. What matters is that he was true to himself, to his calling as a teacher, a rabbi. And so his life and teaching shine out of those dark days, into our own existence, in a calling, commanding manner."[27] "Sainthood is neither sought nor is it to be bestowed."[28] Friedlander finds Baeck remarkably different from so many Jews who, because of events in Nazi Germany, no longer had a religious message and who no longer believed in the "messiah of reason … or the messiah of social progress?…"[29] We must, urges Friedlander, confront men like Baeck. How is that Baeck "…?emerged out of that darkness with his faith intact?"[30] Although his faith was transformed and different, Baeck's faith remained the "faith of Biblical man."[31] Friedlander suggests that Baeck realized man in all his dimensions can only be understood if man is "…?defined as *individuum inaffabile*—man in God's image."[32] This, of course, is part of the reason we believe it is important to perpetuate the memory and legacy of Leo Baeck as he is seen in Sylvanus' play. Our generation, the future generations as well, should be made aware of Baeck's contribution to the dialogue between Jews and Christians. As Friedlander says: "Baeck's discussion of Christianity is a key to his theology and his philosophy of religion. It is also a necessary aspect of the Jewish-Christian dialogue in the twentieth century."[33] Baeck brought "…?a completely new emphasis into the Jewish-Christian dialogue."[34] At this point in the 1990s, as news still continues to come from Germany about rightists and Neo-Nazis, Friedlander is correct in saying "…?the need to understand that land and its relationship to the Jews and Judaism moves into forefront of current issues."[35] We believe Baeck as a person, because of contributions to the encounter between Judaism and Christianity, should be better known and understood. There may be those, as Friedlander points out,[36] within Jewish and Christian communities who have "closed ears" and "closed minds" when it comes to the life of Baeck. Members of the Christian community would be well served to examine what Baeck says in his probing analysis of Christianity, commencing with <u>Das Wesen des Judentums</u> in 1905 and continuing in numerous writings throughout the next fifty or so years.[37] Another example would be his <u>Das Evangelium als Urkunde der jüdischen Glaubensgeschichte</u>, a highly interesting but little-known work published in 1938.

A thorough treatment of Baeck's years in Theresienstadt may also be found in Leonard Baker's <u>Days of Sorrow and Pain</u>.[38] In this book many facts about living conditions in the camp are reported. Baeck's stay began on 28 January 1943. Notwithstanding the statements of some critics that Baeck was "untouched by Theresienstadt,"[38] Baeck himself describes vividly the demeaning and crowded living conditions: "Covering the streets there was … the thick dust that the high ramparts did not keep out and when rain or snow had fallen, there was the deep sticky mud that seemed to grow daily. And from everywhere there came the vermin, a great host—crawling, jumping, flying—in their onslaught against the hungry human beings."[39] Baeck knew, however, that a much more pernicious enemy had to be overcome: "That was the mental fight everyone had to keep up, to see in himself and in his fellow man not only a transport number. It was the fight for the name, one's own and the other's, the fight for individuality, the secret being, one's own and the other's."[40] The inward survival Baeck tried to foster against all odds depended on "patience and imagination."[42] In spite of deplorable conditions people were determined to live in dignity as human beings. This determination was seen in such activities as religious services, lectures, concerts, and theater productions. One of Baeck's great contributions to this effort to humanize the camp conditions was, as mentioned above, his lecture series on Plato, Spinoza, Maimondes, and Kant, as well as on topics like "The Time of the Enlightenment," "The Thoughts of the Nineteenth Century," "Return and Reconciliation," and "Soul and Body."[42] According to Baker, the picture of Baeck that emerges from Theresienstadt is that he was known as a man who could extend comfort merely by his presence, without speaking a word. Since Baeck had many contacts throughout the free world, he often received packages and then shared their contents with his fellow inmates. Baeck officiated, as mentioned above, at many funerals and accompanied processions to the camp enclosures. On one occasion when a Jewish woman's child was going to be aborted by the Nazis in the eighth or ninth month, Leo Baeck interceded, not hesitating to place his prestige and position on the line to confront the Nazis. Sometimes Baeck's greatest service to others was listening and showing understanding. None of Baeck's many lectures in the camp was written down. After liberation Baeck reconstructed a lecture on "The Writing of History," originally delivered in June 1944. He traced the development of history writing, emphasizing the part played by the Greeks and the Israelites. The Greeks, whether Herodotus or Thucydides, wrote of the rise and fall of empires and of the experiences of life, but it was the Jews who wrote of spiritual values, faith, and ideas. The Jewish prophets were opposed to any deeds that could be justified only because of success or expediency. The best life is lived in "justice, goodness, and truth," taught Baeck to the imprisoned Jews. We see the appropriateness of the title of Friedlander's book referred to earlier.

Because there were several hundred Danish Jews in Theresienstadt, the Danish government demanded that the Red Cross be permitted to visit the camp and inspect how inmates were treated. This was in the year 1944 just when the possibility of losing the war was quite apparent to the Germans. Promptly the Nazis decided to make Theresienstadt look like a model camp. Inmates were ordered to scrub and clean the camp before the Red Cross representatives arrived. The camp commandant, Karl Rahm, gave orders through Jewish representative that Jews were not to mention true living conditions. Baeck described the disappointment of the visit: The Red Cross "…?appeared to be completely taken in by the false front put up for their benefit."[43] Baeck described the disappointment felt by the Jews that the Red Cross commission seemed uninterested in learning the truth. No one took the trouble to walk upstairs in the buildings where masses of people were crowded together. From the streets the ground floors looked orderly and attractive. A camp orchestra prepared a program for the Red Cross officials and continued to perform thereafter. Baeck, however, was so angered at the presentation of the visit that he boycotted the concerts.

Where were inmates headed after Theresienstadt and what did Baeck know about their fate? To answer these questions is to look at a sensitive issue Baeck had to deal with, and also to look at vulnerable areas in Baeck's character, which critics have sharply attacked. Auschwitz was the destination "to the east" for many of the deportees. The horror of Auschwitz, as Baker observes,[44] is not alone the numbers. The ultimate horror is how technological perfection was used to make killing masses of human beings seem like a "statistical event."[45] By August 1943, after arriving in January, Baeck heard the first reliable report of what was happening in Auschwitz. Baeck reported after the war that a half-Jew escaped from Auschwitz and sent a message to Baeck in Theresienstadt. Baeck responded: "So it is not just a rumor, as I had hoped, or the illusion of a diseased imagination."[46] What effect did this knowledge have on Baeck? He decided, as Baker says, "to tell no one." This was, for his critics, the "grave decision." Sylvanus, in Scene VII, presents the factual basics: "Man weiß, wohin sie gebracht werden. Rabbi Baeck weiß es auch." Baeck continued his routines of visiting people, chatting with friends, caring for children, and lecturing on the lofty ideals of religion and history. The German theologian Paul Tillich criticized Baeck for withholding truth, implying that such behavior is synonymous with not telling the terminally ill patient the full truth."[47] Friedlander, whose study was cited above, offers the explanation that Baeck not only for the sake of morale in the camp wanted to avoid spreading the information, but also because he may have been reluctant to spread a story whose accuracy he may have doubted.[48] H. G. Alder, an inmate who knew Baeck well, survived and wrote an account of life in the camp. He was in disagreement with Baeck's reasoning for not saying more. "…?the general lack of information about the true fate of all those who went from Theresienstadt to the death camps of the east led to thoughtlessness and self-deception which was barely limited by darkening of consciousness."[49] In the last months before liberation the Council of Elders was so depleted that Baeck was finally selected to become a member, eventually becoming Chief Elder. He viewed his main task as one of maintaining the morale of the few remaining Jews.

Hannah Arendt, in her book <u>Eichmann in Jerusalem</u>,[50] aroused considerable hostility in the Reform and Liberal Jewish communities because of her criticism of Baeck. Assuming that Baeck made his decision for "humane" reasons, Arendt argues that, as one witness of the Eichmann trial said, "…?people volunteered for deportations from Theresienstadt to Auschwitz and denounced those who tried to tell them the truth as 'not sane.'"[51] It is likely that Arendt was influenced in her criticism of Baeck by several factors such as trial testimony, by Raul Hilberg's <u>The Destruction of the European Jews</u>, as well as by Blumenfeld who wrote that "Baeck war ein durch und durch verlogener Bursche, aber er hatte Mut."[52] After the publication of <u>Eichmann in Jerusalem</u> and after her series in the <u>New Yorker</u>, Arendt received support for her criticism from Reha Freier, the founder of the organization that became Youth Aliyah.[53] Arendt's view of Baeck is not, however, one-sided. Her written remarks on Baeck had a certain irony and lack of balance, according to young-Bruehl.[54] Her admiration for Baeck was expressed in 1963 to a student group at Columbia University when Baeck's former student Alfred Friedlander invited her to speak. Friedlander noted: "For more than two hours she answered questions clearly and cogently, displaying her knowledge and awareness of Jewish and general history. She showed warm feelings toward the Jewish and general history. She showed warm feelings towards the Jewish people and their tragic position during the Hitler days, and supplemented some portions of her book (viz. she lauded Leo Baeck highly)."[55]

When Rabbi Wolli Kaelter was asked about the attacks by Arendt and others on Leo Baeck, he stated that the believed Baeck acted as he did truly out of regard for others. He grants that Baeck was making a compromise. Kaelter believes the criticisms of Arendt are not shared by those who knew Baeck well. "Leo Baeck was one of the most towering men of the twentieth century," asserts Kaelter.

As indicated above by several quotations, we have had the rare privilege of conducting personal interviews with three men in the Los Angeles area who knew Leo Baeck in one capacity or another. You our readers may be interested in their connection to Baeck's legacy.

From 1930 on Baeck was serving and teaching at the <u>Hochschule für die Wissenschaft des Judentums</u> in Berlin. Among the students were Alfred Friedlander, Alfred Wolf, Wolli Kaelter, and Bert Woythaler. One day a letter from America arrived with an announcement that scholarships and study opportunities were available for five rabbinical students. Prof. Elbogen made the administrative decisions. Rabbi Alfred Wolf, for nearly forty years serving in the Wilshire Boulevard Temple in the Wilshire district of Los Angeles, was one of the five selected to go. He vividly remembered departing Germany on 5 September 1935, as we sat talking in his office. By 1948 Wolf was regional director in the Los Angeles area for the Union of American Hebrew Congregations. On one occasion he invited Baeck to come to Los Angeles to speak. Wolf inquired if Baeck had any special requests while in Los Angeles. Baeck said he had two. First, he wanted to call on a lady who had been his housekeeper. Wolf found it so characteristic of Baeck that, instead of announcing himself and waiting to see who may come, he took the initiative to look up and call on the lady. Second, Baeck said he would like to visit the ocean. Did anything remarkable happen? Wolf was convinced it was a truly "spiritual experience" for Baeck, though he confides it would be difficult to explain what he means by "spiritual experience." The question has sometimes been raised as to what extent Baeck accommodated the Nazis. When seen in a larger context, states Wolf, this is exactly parallel to what had happened for 2000 years in one form or another: compromise or perish! Baeck, of course, did not convert, but he was concerned with honorable survival. Baeck, in his presentation of new ideas, was reminiscent of Moses Mendelssohn in the eighteenth century. Baeck had an interest in multiculturism. Wolf believes the explanation for this interest was Baeck's vast knowledge of ancient and many modern cultures. Collectivism also played a role in Baeck's thinking. And how did the individual arrive at an identification? Baeck's answer, according to Wolf, was to know the past and to respond to it.

Rabbi Wolli Kaelter of Long Beach, California, who serves as a part-time professor at Hebrew Union College of Rabbinic Studies, was another one of the five students sent to America in 1935.[56] Kaelter remembers his mother was opposed to the idea in the first place. Her husband had died several years earlier when Kaelter was a lad. To ease the pain of departure he promised his mother he would return to Germany. By the time young Kaelter returned in May 1936 he observed some ominous differences to which some Jews seemed oblivious.

Kaelter was acquainted with Baeck not only because he had audited a homiletics course taught by Baeck, but also because Baeck was his father's friend. What childhood memories did he have of Baeck? Baeck was occasionally a quest in the Kaelter home in Danzig. One time a dessert was served that could be topped with chocolate sauce. Each person's dish was an elegant bowl with delicate filigree design around the edge. Rabbi Baeck placed his bowl nearer the chocolate and proceeded to serve himself. Baeck put so much sauce in his dish that it began overflowing through the filigree design. The youngsters were highly amused when Baeck picked up his bowl under which was a perfect circle of chocolate drippings! Rabbi Kaelter told of another memory of Baeck on the ligher side. One of Baeck's former students resided in Danzig. His house was an elegant villa with many valuable and delicate art works on display in the entry hall. Rabbi Baeck was invited to use the house and had a key to enter. However, when he arrived at the house it was night. He was told to be aware of the artwork on display. Because of his poor eyesight he was afraid of walking through the entry hall so he proceeded to crawl through on his hands and knees until he was upstairs! Such memories serve to point out lesser-known personality traits of a man who otherwise leave the public awe-struck.

In our efforts to trace down other people in the Los Angeles area who knew Leo Baeck, we also had an interview with Rabbi Bert Woythaler of San Fernando Valley.[57] As a voucher of his contact with Baeck he showed us his course book from the <u>Hochschule für die Wissenschaft des Judentums</u> in Berlin with Baeck's signature. When the letter from America came asking for rabbinical students, Wythaler also conceded, it was actually Prof. Elbogen who made the administrative decision, rather than Baeck. Woythaler remained in the United States and graduated in 1940 from the Rabbinican Seminary in New York. His memory of Baeck is that of a soft-spoken person. He was, as mentioned above, no great orator. Although Woythaler identifies himself more with the Conservative movement, whereas it is mainly the Reform movement in the United States that takes note of Baeck. In his concluding remarks Rabbi Woythaler said he believes it is an "impoverishment" if one does not know of Baeck's life and work.

In this attempt to revive or at least to get in contact with the legacy of Leo Baeck we have, up to this point, consulted several sources. Among them were, most importantly, articles and books written by people who personally knew Back. Likewise we had interviews with several people who contributed anecdotes and recollections from memories of Baeck. No doubt some of these memories are now for the first time being committed to writing and preserved for posterity. Whether you are making a first acquaintance with Baeck, or perhaps renewing a longstanding acquaintance, it is our hope that the information will contribute to a deeper appreciation of Baeck the man as well as of the present work about his life.

2

Perhaps an explanation of how this project got started would be of interest to our readers. In 1985 Robert Rhée was visiting Germany in and around Dortmund where he and his family lived before emigrating in 1936. In his search for records of family history in Westphalia he came across Hans C. Meyer's <u>Aus Geschichte und Leben der Juden in Westfalen</u>. In the appendix a text caught his attention. It was not a text on family history. Rather it was a text entitled "Leo Baeck. Eine Hörfolge nach authentischen Texten." A footnote added: "Vorabdruck aus dem Manuskript. Alle Rechte liegen beim Verfasser!" Born in Soest but reared in Dortmund, Erwin Sylvanus (1917-1985) was the author. More on account of Rabbi Baeck's name in the title than on account of Erwin Sylvanus' name Rhée decided the text may deserve more attention. Back home in Malibu, California, Rhée commenced translating the German text into English. In the early part of 1987 he sought advice and help in the translation from a native Berliner who is a professor at Pepperdine University in Malibu. For one reason or another the professor declined, but recommended that Robert Rhée should contact the present writer. This he did. One day my office telephone rang. Thus began my involvement with this project. When asked if I knew anything about Rabbi Baeck or had any interest in him, I said I knew about him through his famous <u>Das Wesen des Judentums</u> and that I was interested in him for a couple of other reasons. Baeck spent a major portion of his career in Berlin. I had studied at the Free University of Berlin and Berlin is where Moses Mendelssohn was active during the eighteenth century. (Mendelssohn was the focus of some research I had been doing for several years.) It wasn't long before Robert Rhée and I were meeting regularly and our friendship grew. By the time I had complete translations of difficult passages and revising major portions of the text, the fiftieth anniversary of that dark date in German history, 9 November 1938, was approaching. Actor/director Jeff Cory and writer Tony van Reterghem prepared an abridged version of the text. The Jewish Community Center and Synagogue of Malibu as well as the Leo Baeck Temple of Los Angeles, of which Robert Rhée is a member, used the abridged text for the public performances of the piece. Since that time it has been our earnest desire to have the text published and to have it produced as a docudrama on videotape.

John Gross, reviewing Steven Spielberg's film <u>Schindler's List</u> (<u>The New York Review</u>, 3 February 1994, pp. 14-16), poses the question of how many holocaust films the mass public can absorb. He writes "Holocaust denial may or may not be a major problem in the future, but Holocaust ignorance, Holocaust forgetfulness, and Holocaust indifference are bound to be,?…" (p. 16) Gross is convinced that such contributions to popular culture as Spielberg's film will do much to dispel ignorance. As the world enters the final years of the 1990s, and soon also the twenty-first century, it is necessary and incumbent upon us to keep alive the memories of events that draw upon and illustrate the historical, cultural, and religious reservoirs of a man like Baeck. We are now living in the time Baeck foresaw when there would be more dialogue between Judaism and Christianity. Baeck saw the relationship between parent and child. Judaism as well as Christianity should listen to what Baeck had to say. We offer Sylvanus' treatment as an important way of hearing part of what Baeck had to say. Eliezer Berkovits said Jews are the ones "…?in whose martyrdom Christianity suffered its worst moral debacle." In spite of, and maybe because of, many anniversaries and works about the Holocaust, we believe that there exists a need in both Jewish and non-Jewish communities to cast another in-depth look at, and recall, the human dilemmas that faced the victims of the Holocaust; dilemmas which, to a lesser degree, also face us in dealing with the political and humanitarian problems of today and of the coming twenty-first century. In so doing it will also keep alive not only the memories of events, but the very Judeo-Christian awareness of honesty, truth, and compassion.

3

The specific reason is yet to be discovered why Sylvanus, in those post-war years in Germany, was driven to write a work on Rabbi Leo Baeck. There is no doubt, however, that the character and wisdom of Baeck attracted him. Sylvanus (3 October 1917—17 November 1985) spent his early years growing up in Dortmund,[58] also the hometown of co-translator Robert Rhée. During his teenage years he wrote poems in the spirit of Nazism. He wrote and published while in military service (Der ewige Krieg, 1941, and Der ewige Dichterkreis, 1943). He returned from the war seriously wounded. More and more during the 1950s he devoted himself to writing for radio and television. His main purpose was to combat hatred, brutality, and inhumanity.[59] An international success was his 1957 play Korczak und die Kinder, which brought him the Leo-Baeck-Preis in 1959. A question, which still must remain unanswered, is which came first, the Leo-Baeck-Preis or the play Leo Baeck? He was also honored with the Jochen-Klepper-Medaille in 1960 as well as with the Hoseph-Winkler-Stiftung in 1961.

A thematic relationship exists between Sylvanus' Leo Baeck and Korczak und die Kinder. The later (called a "szenisches Requiem" by the Spiegel reviewer[60]) tells the story of the Jewish physician Dr. Janusz Korczak, director of an orphanage in the Warsaw Ghetto, who refuses to forsake his charges and goes voluntarily with them to Maidanek. The 1950s, as Hellmuth Karasek states,[61] were characterized by "vergangenheitsbewältigende Stüke." Of course, one of the most difficult topics was the racial genocide of the Jews. Karasek believes that perhaps in the clearest manner Sylvanus' piece shows the difficulties and questions that could arise with this topic. (Sylvanus' work Korczak was the first one to appear on the topic after the dramatized version of Diary of Anne Frank.) Less a plot than anything else, Korczak may be regarded as a type of "memento," as a report in the style of the scene epic of Brecht. It attempts to stir up lukewarm people and combat the shameful, brazen forgetfulness of the Germans.[62] One reviewer finds Sylvanus' style shockingly tactless, not because of evil intentions, but more result of naiveté.[63] This same reviewer has serious reservations about who should actually treat such a topic, or who should actually perform it, and in what style it should be written. Implicit in these questions is the conviction that Sylvanus should not have written it, and the style should have been more elevated for it truly to be a memento. The factor of contemporary public opinion, says Schulze-Vellinghausen, in a sense removed it as unsuitable from the realm of the theater. In a manner of reminiscent of funeral scenes, the spectators were compelled after the first performance to depart the theater without applause. Notwithstanding these criticisms and reservations, <u>Korczak und die Kinder</u> became an international success.

In 1959, Sylvanus presented the less-successful theater prize <u>Zwi Worte töten</u> in Göttingen. This piece is thematically not quite so directly related to the above two. According to the <u>Spiegel</u> review, Sylvanus develops and employs a new theatrical method called "tachistische Dramaturgie."[64] The term is derived from the French "la tache" (the spot) and was originally used to refer to the technique of certain modern painters who tried to produce effects by painting with spots and colored sprays. "Durch eine Vielzahl von Szenenfetzen soll dabei die Wirklichkeit vorgeführt und aus ihr eine erkennbare, moralische Struktur herausgehoben werden."[65] As in the present text, and in <u>Korczak und die Kinder</u>, Sylvanus uses a real event for <u>Zwei worte töten</u>. On New Year's Eve, 31 December 1957, in the Westphalian town of Soest (Sylvanus' birthplace) a black Canadian soldier stabbed a twenty-year-old German youth. The soldier and his German girl friend leave a bar. Drunken teenagers yell "Du Negerhure," the so-called two words that kill alluded to by the title. A German woman stuck her head out the window, said, "Damit wollen wir nichts zu tun haben!", and slammed the window shut. The soldier drew a knife and attacked an innocent bystander who was actually the only person trying to calm the turmoil. Obviously Sylvanus is treating the theme of hatred and is preaching a moral lesson. The <u>Spiegel</u> reviewer suggests that all characters are victims in some way—victims of social prejudices, of governmental-political crimes, of the indifferent environment. The girl in the story was apparently forced to become a prostitute when she lost her parents while fleeing East Prussia. The black soldier was reared by a merciless father who forced his son into a hostile white society. Even the violence of the rowdy teenagers is supposedly explained by Sylvanus as the effects of the war with its brutalities such as concentration camps and as the effect of daily life in West Germany. It appears as though in the end all the characters are innocent, whereas the "innocent" audience is supposed to depart feeling guilty. "…?die Zuschauer [mußten] zur Besinnung kommen und den Wunsch haben, ein besseresLeben zu führen." (<u>Spiegal</u>, p. 58) The thematic differences between <u>Zwei Worte töten</u> and <u>Leo Baeck</u> are obvious. This will be discussed more later.

The entire context in which Sylvanus is working—Vergangenheitsbewältigung—was bustling with other attempts to deal with the past and to preach moral lessons. Probably the best-known example of this type of literature was Frisch's Audorra. Peter Weiss, in his Ermittlung, used the technique of a "documentary" to show that no stage version could do justice to the incongruencies of Auschwitz. Thomas Harlan's Ich selbst und kein Engel, memorialized an unknown hero of the Warsaw Ghetto. Similar works from the period were Hans Breinlinger's Konzert an der Memel and Johannes Becher's Winterschlacht. These last two works share in common the theme of a German soldier who prefers being killed rather than to participate in killing Russian Jews. In Kein Zeit für Heilige, by Joachim Wickman, the theme of unredeemed guilt for crimes against Jews is treated. Johannes Mario Simmel's Schulfreund describes the fate of a letter carrier, once a schoolmate of Göring's, who hides a Jew but is declared insane and loses his retirement.[66]

The style employed by Sylvanus in Leo Baeck manifests itself from the beginning: "Die Geschichte des jüdischen Volkes zählt weit über 5000 Jahre." These words are intoned not by one of the characters, but by a "Speaker." The audience cannot escape the impression that the first thirty lines are a straightforward historical account or report. Particular attention is paid to numbers and dates. This same style and approach are continued consistently in almost all ten scenes. More than 5000 years of Jewish history are alluded to in the first sentence. The covenant between God and the Jewish people seems to be of central importance for explaining the existence of the Jews as well as of their teachers and sages. Interwoven into Jewish history, says the speaker, is the history of persecution. Sylvanus uses the information about dates to come in an oblique manner to that fateful date "nach dem christlichen Kalender—30 January 1933. It is the year 5693 according to the Jewish calendar.

The entire piece, in summary, consists of ten scenes, numbered I—X. Each of the ten scenes opens with a "Speaker" giving a precise historical date. As observed above, this "tachistische Dramaturgie" with fragmentary scenes is employed to evoke reality and imply moral structure. By Scene III, a chronological sequence is clear. Anticipation and suspense begin mounting since it is, by Scene III, the early months of 1938 and Baeck is in Munich at a meeting of the Organization of Rabbis. Suspense is heightened as Rabbi Neumeyer is ordered to enter a waiting police car. For the first time a Nazi stormtrooper makes an appearance. Neumeyer returns and tells of the Nazis' plans to destroy the synagogue. Baeck, Neumeyer, and the students debate the merits of protesting the planned destruction.

Between Scenes III and IV, the destructive tragedy of Kristallnacht had occurred. Sylvanus omits a direct portrayal, which is what we would expect stylistically. For a Hollywood or other sensational version of this period, such an omission by Sylvanus would be considered inadmissible. We can only speculate that for audiences of Sylvanus' time—be they film, radio, or theater audiences—presentation of such harsh realities would have been inappropriate. How is a stage contrivance supposed to make events like Auschwitz comprehensible? "Die Betroffenheit war an größten." "Das schwierigste Thema," writes Hellmuth Karasek, "innerhalb der vergangenheitsbewältigenden Stücke bildete der Völkermord an den Juden."[67] Baeck and Neumeyer discuss whether it is better to stay or leave. Baeck expresses his resolve to stay in Germany as long as there is still one Jew left. Neumeyer's arguments are to no avail. Neumeyer is determined to leave and Baeck encourages him to leave with all good conscience. After all, had Neumeyer not heroically pressed for justice in a case filed against the SS trooper for brutally shooting down a Jewish prisoner in the year 1933 in Dachau?

In Scene V, the stormtrooper arrives to arrest Dr. Baeck. Sylvanus uses this scene to represent the snide attitude, propagated within the last six years by the Nazis through schoolteachers, toward Jewish aspects of the Bible. Jewish prophets, says the stormtrooper, are foreign; "…?we no longer need time … we are Aryans." As if to give a glimpse into a compassionate corner of the stormtrooper's heart, Sylvanus has his say, "I always think such an old Jew, as painless as possible.…" In these parting moments, Baeck is shown as being concerned about bills and obligations. Of this particular scene from Baeck's life Ruth Klüger writes, "…?von dem ich spatter mit Beremden las, er habe noch seine Gasrechnung bezahlt, als die Ausheber, die Schergen, vor der Tür seiner Berliner Wohnung standen, ihn abzuholen. Wollte er einen guten Eindruck hinterlassen, Risches vermindern, bevor man ihn abschleppte? Schildbürger waren die Juden, wie sie das Licht aus Säcken im finstern Rathaus ausgossen."[68] Baeck is thoughtful enough to say farewell to his housekeeper, to dispense words of encouragement. "Trust Him, to whom time belongs.…"

Scene VI opens with Baeck in Theresienstadt, where he was part of a two-man team with the Dutch professor of philosophy Dr. Bousemaa. Although physically under great strain as they hauled garbage from the camp, Baeck and Bousemaa occupied their minds with discussions about God and holiness. Sylvanus interjects chidings from a stormtrooper who wants them to work faster and keep in step. Once again, as in the previous scene, a note of compassion seems to be struck by the stormtrooper; after scolding Baeck and Bousemaa, he says to himself, "My God, I am not subhuman. Tomorrow I've got to line up 650. It's getting faster by the week … and simpler."

It is 1944 as Scene VII opens. At this point Sylvanus begins honing in on the tragic facts of the past ("…?more and more people, defenseless and helpless …

will be gassed, killed. Because they are Jews. No other reason. ("Human brains invented the gas chambers.") and the present ("Human brains of people who were neighbors, and perhaps are still neighbors. We don't want to deny it…. "). Without a doubt at this point Sylvanus was getting next to his German audience. As Walter Olma states, "…?auf der Bühne engagierte er sich gegen Haß, Gewalt, Willkürlichkeit und Unmenschlichkeit."[69] Albert Schulze-Vellinghausen's comment on Korczak und die Kinder could just as well be said of Leo Baeck: "Das Werk … soll die Lauen rühren und gegen unser aller schmachvoll-schamlose Vergeßlichkeit kämpfen."[70] Sylvanus was treading on thin ice and making himself vulnerable to criticism. Once again, words originally said regarding Korczak und die Kinder seem applicable to Leo Baeck. Hellmuth Karasek believed "…?daß der Autor die ehrenvolle Aufgabe übernommen habe, die Erinnerungen an schmachvolled Unrecht wachzuhalten."[71] Some of the dialogue here between Baeck and the inmates belies the criticisms of Hannah Arendt. Death seems inevitable for all deportees. Baeck knows it and the inmates know it. Sylvanus deepens the atmosphere of pathos when eighteen-year-old Michael, a lonely orphan, comes on the scene and implores Baeck to send him on the next deportation. Baeck, trying to help Michael examine his motives, asks "You did not come to me out of pride? Or because you are tired? Or because you are disgusted? Or for fear of the continuous fear? I could understand it, Michael. I wish that you just stay alive … here … with me … even if it is only a short time … that also takes courage, Michael."

It is April 1945 as Scene VIII opens and Baeck is in solitary confinement. Baeck occupies himself with writing the manuscript of This People Israel. At the moment he finished the words "He [Moses] created this nation for the mission?…" an SS officer's voice resounds with a command. Eichmann, that dealer of death, is face to face with Baeck. The facts of that almost miraculous sparing of Baeck's life are disclosed: Nazi records listed a Rabbi Beck, spelled B E C K, as being long dead. Eichmann seals Baeck's fate. He is doomed to be deported in two or three days. Baeck has only two requests: "Can I finish a few things?" "Can Michael be with me once more?" Eichmann agrees, saying in a hauntingly hollow sentence "We are not subhuman." Momentarily Michael appears for three minutes. Baeck commits to his loyal care wedding rings, letters, and the unfinished manuscript. When Michael's turn comes he should commit it all to another friend's care.

After a few facts about the last years of Baeck's life in London, the brief Scene X presents Baeck first reading from the last chapter of This People Israel. It is that passage about the importance of living unselfishly. Then a female (housekeeper?)

comes in with a letter from Germany. Baeck is invited to come and speak at a convention. Will he go? He says he will not refuse. They want to make a new beginning; he has many friends among the Germans. The German-Jewish symbiosis was long a pet idea of his. Sylvanus puts almost incredible words into Baeck's mouth: "It was not their fault that they could not prevent this misfortune...." Baeck mentions the pious Christians who also perished. His indomitable spirit of optimism shines forth. Baeck will go and speak because he believes the Germans can learn gratitude from the Jews. Maimonides is the topic of his address. Many great Germans intersect in their admiration for Maimonides. The future, assures Baeck, is blessed only when people have learned to be kind, just, and unselfish. All this would seem contrived by Sylvanus, were it not for the overwhelming confirming evidence that shows these to be the true sentiments of Baeck in the postwar years. "I want to be able," said German President Theodor Heuss as quoted by Sylvanus, "to express how beautiful, how right, indeed how necessary I consider it that this picture of his [Baeck's] is presented to a wider consciousness and will be guaranteed."

In conclusion, let it be observed that Sylvanus as a writer presents little more than the facts. He knew his limitations within the format of a radio play. His style is simple, direct, and dignified. It is as though he is giving a report. If there is dramatic action or suspense it is because the real events were dramatic and suspenseful. Actual scenes of death and destruction do not occur. In a sense the play hardly qualifies as a Hollywood "Holocaust thriller." Such a category is well represented by the 1978 television series Holocaust or most recently by Spielberg's Schindler's List. Not to be forgotten are such towering documentary films as Lanzmanns's Shoah and Ophuls' Hotel Terminus. But, for historical reasons alone, it is noteworthy that Sylvanus made this modest contribution to our understanding of the Holocaust and a man of Baeck's stature. Sylvanus was a non-Jew, yet he was apparently deeply intrigued by the tragic chapter in human history written by the Nazis. (He himself had at one time been tinged by the spirit of Nazism and had served as a Nazi officer.) He believed, possibly, that all this was a phenomenon that had to be confronted by the German public. It is not as though he were preaching to the Germans or castigating them. There is no discussion of guilt. (In Scene VII he raised the possibility that some of the murderers may still be neighbors.) He simply presents spots or flashes of past events that should not be forgotten or hidden. Sylvanus does not employ artistic creativity to present Baeck's life to his audience. Rather, he allows a portrait of Baeck to emerge that is, according to the subtitle, based to a large extent on Baeck's own published and unpublished theological writings. Precisely which passages from which works he quotes Sylvanus never discloses. Some of Baeck's statements have the ring of passages in his famous <u>Das Wesen des Judentums</u>, although it is difficult to pinpoint which ones they are.

LEO BAECK
A DIALOGUE BASED ON
AUTHENTIC TEXTS

(abridged)
by Erwin Sylvanus

Voices: Speaker

                 Leo Baeck

                 Alfred Neumeyer

                 Commander

                 Bousemaa

                 Michael

                 An S.S. leader

                 Russian colonel

                 Adolf Eichmann

                 A female voice

                 Several male voices

I

(Introductory Music)

Speaker: It was the third day of the fifth month Sch'wath of the year 5693 of the Jewish calendar. In Germany, it was January 30, 1933. Rabbi Leo Baeck, president of the Organization of Rabbis in Germany, was giving a lecture to his students.

Leo Baeck: … in the Greek language, the word law, "nomos" describes something functional within an entirety. In

24

this one word is brought together: law, creation, and revelation. They are the same, as God's "covenant." This word once meant contract. Contract changed into law which includes creation and revelation.

(students begin muttering)

My dear students, your inappropriate unrest forces me to interrupt my lecture. May I know why you are disrupting?

First Voice: Rabbi Baeck, please excuse us, but an hour ago the president nominated Adolf Hitler as chancellor.

Third Voice: My father tells me we have to expect the worst....

Second Voice: Nonsense. Don't take the Nazis seriously.

Fourth Voice: They are anti-Semitic racists!

Anti-Semites. That's an anachronism in this century. They cannot turn back progress, erase the Enlightenment....

Fifth Voice: This cannot simply exclude a group of legitimate German citizens! A part of the population.

Leo Baeck: My dear, young friends. I can understand your concern and certainly excuse the urgent interruption. But, it is no time to give up on our rights. To the contrary, this is a time when we have to be conscious of our legacy of the law.

Third Voice: Nazis don't care about rights and justice....

Leo Baeck: Behind our rights stands the One who revealed them. They do not need any other protection. We know already from Maimonides that our rights do not require power to be right and to shine before us. Maimonides left his home in Spain; for many years he was a fugitive in Northern Africa. A fugitive, our great teacher of the Law. And if you want to get an answer to this news which has shocked you so much we turn to the writings of Maimonides. Just the title "Moreh Nebuchim" gives direction and support for those who waver ... Guide for the lost....

First Voice: Rabbi Baeck, you know our regard for you, you know of our observance of the law, our law. But we also owe allegiance to the country where we were born and grew up. We are German Jews.... The law of the state is also religious law.

Leo Baeck: I know, young friend, this is what the Talmud teaches. I was chaplain during the first World War. I volunteered?...

First Voice: We love Germany. But, now it does not love <u>us</u> anymore. A conflict is unavoidable.

Leo Baeck: I want to answer you with a statement I made seven years ago to my esteemed colleague, Rabbi Seligmann. We belong to the realm of the state and the realm of God. Which laws should they follow more when there is a conflict? Where this spiritual conflict exits, there can come a time where a stand has to be taken, for the worldly or the eternal. To make this choice means to be ready to be a martyr, to recognize religion and its laws, above all. Dear friends take this as my position to the sobering new with which you interrupted me.

(fade out)

Speaker: The boards of the Jewish communities in Germany were called to a meeting a few weeks later. This emergency group of the "Governmental Representatives of the German Jews" elected Leo Baeck as its chair and spokesperson.

Leo Baeck:

Fifth Voice: We have to leave Germany. Better today than tomorrow.

Leo Baeck: I don't consider it irresponsible if a Jew in Germany now decides to leave the country.

Third Voice: It is impossible for all of us to leave.

Leo Baeck:	The greater part will be unable to leave. However, we should suggest to our young people to leave—most occupations are already closed to them. Let us tell of the travels of our ancestors and Palestine....
Fifth Voice:	What about the elderly? What will happen to them? I love Germany. I will stay.
Leo Baeck:	Yes, we Jews have deeper roots than the others. In religion. We are the people of God. That's why the conflict has hit us stronger and more often—the tragedy in the elevated sense, tragedy through which history become spiritual and great?...

(fade out)

II

(Musical Introduction)

Speaker:	It was now five years later, at the end of the year 5698 of the Jewish calendar. There had been programs; soon it would be "Kristallnacht," the night of broken glass, where all Jewish store windows were smashed. Rabbi Baeck was addressing a meeting of the Organization of Rabbis in Munich when he was handed a noted with an order: Chief Justice Neumeyer was to immediately take a waiting police car to the Department for Jewish Affairs at the Ministry of the Interior, there to receive information.
Neumeyer:	It is not the first time that they call me ... but I was never called under such circumstances.
Leo Baeck:	They don't respect me either. It is forbidden, according to the Nurnberg Laws, that any German citizen have, or show the respect for, a Jew.
Second Voice:	At least they still address you.
Leo Baeck:	Only because I live in Munich under the eyes of the world and because the foreign countries observe my

appearances before the representatives of the German government.

First Voice: We could have left the country three years ago ... now it is too late ... One has to be rich, very rich....

Stormtrooper: I've been ordered to take the Jew Neumeyer to the Commissioner. NOW! ... Where is he ... Have him come out ... I don't enter your synagogues!

Neumeyer: I am retired Chief Justice Alfred Neumeyer. Please, let us both go. May I bring my associate?

Leo Baeck: I am the chairman of the Organization of Jews in Germany, Rabbi Baeck, and would?...

Stormtrooper: No. Only the chief Jew of Munich.... No one else. Come on ... it won't take long. Hurry up.

Neumeyer: Shalom.

Stormtrooper: (suspicious) What's that you said?

Neumeyer: Our greeting ... Shalom. That means peace.

(Stormtrooper raises his eyebrows and grins)

Speaker: The stormtrooper escorted Dr. Neumeyer out. Hours later, Dr. Neumeyer was returned to the meeting and made his report.

Neumeyer: I will have to tell you—all of you: This synagogue, our synagogue, will be destroyed, torn down, they say, by tomorrow. Hitler himself gave the order. He was here yesterday ... as he drove to the House of Arts he gave the order?...

First Voice: The Holy Scrolls of Scripture are in danger ... where shall we store them?

Leo Baeck: May I know the reason, Dr. Neumeyer?

Neumeyer: "Reason?" The growing traffic requires the destruction of this synagogue in the center of Munich. That is the "reason."

Leo Baeck:	Do you have a written order?
Neumeyer:	No. The official did not even receive me personally. It was settled in the hall. "The order should suffice," he said. An appeal would be useless, they could tell me that now. They would start with the demolition tomorrow?...
Third Voice:	That is the beginning ... of the end of the Jews in Munich.
Neumeyer:	The Bavarian Ministry of the Interior acquires the property. That means we have to sell the synagogue. They prepare a contract, and we have to sign. That is how they maintain the appearance of justice. The sale price is set by the Ministry, a ridiculous price ... but that is not the question at the moment.
Leo Baeck:	The synagogue is a symbol. Until now, they only required the segregation of the Jewish people. Now they also want ... the synagogue ... our God. I have to return to Munich. But I don't want to leave without finishing my lecture, the last lecture of a rabbi in this revered synagogue, where Jews prayed, sang, and celebrated their high holidays for the last 50 years. The time when we will have to live alone from our teachings, without ceremonies; it seems to be closer than we expected, due to vicious force. Dear Dr. Neumeyer, please be seated. I will be finished in a few minutes. Much becomes superfluous which otherwise could have been said.

The Jew always wanted to be as Jew: the greater nonconformist in history, the great dissenter. That was their calling. The fight for religion had to be a fight for self-preservation for this reason. It did not include an idea of power, it would have been a contradiction—not power, but individuality, personality for the sake of God. Not power, but strength. Jewish existence is as strength in this world. And strength is greatness?...

(fade out)

III

Speaker:	It was not until a year later in 1939 that Rabbi Leo Baeck and Judge Neumeyer would meet again in Munich, at the end of the year 5699 of the Jewish calendar. The great synagogues of Germany were no more. Kristallnacht had brought the planned burning and destruction of German synagogues. The World Union of Progressive Judaism had elected Rabbi Leo Baeck as its chair—as symbol of its respect for the leader of the persecuted and disgraced German Jews. The rabbi was sitting in front of the first pages of the manuscript of his intended book, This People of Israel. He wanted to begin the second chapter, when Judge Neumeyer entered his study.
Neumeyer:	(enters) Greetings.
Leo Baeck:	Shalom, my dear Judge Neumeyer, you finally could make your trip.
Neumeyer:	I had to wait for permission.... in order to travel from Munich to Berlin ... seven months....
Leo Baeck:	How is the Jewish Community?
Neumeyer:	Confused and frightened, but still hopeful.... looking towards you, Rabbi Baeck. They do not want to believe that even you can no longer help.
Leo Baeck:	My life is equally threatened. I was ordered for questioning three times ... they wanted to accuse me of treasonous acts. My appointment to a foreign Jewish aid organization fanned their hatred. I was informed this morning that it would be better for me to leave the country. They want to get rid of me. They even offered to waive the emigration taxes. They are willing to forgo this money.
Neumeyer:	And you are sitting at your desk....

Leo Baeck:	I have planned this book for years. A book that will give witness of Jewish existence, today and forever. In Germany and everywhere.
Neumeyer:	We are mocked and despised. Nobody wants anything to do with us. How smart were those who left Germany long ago … this country, and these people we loved, and that now kick us. And you, Rabbi Baeck, write a book in the German language, which no German is allowed to print, no German may buy, or would like to read, or be allowed to read, and?…
Leo Baeck:	"We were slaves to Pharaoh in Egypt, and God led us from there. The One who is, our God, with a strong hand …"
Neumeyer:	We should leave Germany, you and I.
Leo Baeck:	I do not read these instructions in the sacred words. I read that our ancestors led out of Egypt according to the oath of the One who is. The Jews in Germany are not the entire Jewish people. Palestine will not accept all of us … the British do not want it. I have to stay as long as one Jew remains in Germany?…
Neumeyer:	The Hebrew University in Jerusalem offered you a chair. And you may leave without a head tax. They ask a high price for me. Almost my entire assets. I intended to stay with my congregation. But, it makes no sense. I would only add to the victims. I am an attorney. At the inception of the brown shirt government, I thought that Germany would soon return to respect for the law. I was wrong. A large part of the population in Germany does not recognize law and justice. Rabbi, you're sacrificing yourself senselessly. Take the chance, leave the country…. You will be received with honors. I beg you … as Jew, and as friend.
Leo Baeck:	I can understand, but bring my greetings to the Jews outside. But I'll stay … You worked for the law courageously—the inalienable rights of the Jews as part of the

rights of humanity. Among my papers is a copy of your letter of March 31, 1933, a document of justice, dignity, and humanity?...

Speaker: (reads) To his Excellency, Secretary General von Epp, Munich. We strongly protest against the attack directed against us. We German Jews always worked for Germany. In World War I thousands of us gave their lives. The welfare of our country was always our highest goal. We cannot, and do not ever want, to oppose the measures taken against us. But we will steadfastly endure them with the knowledge that we are exposed to a great injustice. The heavenly being, ruler of the world, will give us strength. We pray to God, to give our German friends the insight that the road to the national reconstruction of Germany does not require the suppression of the Jews?...

Neumeyer: That was six years ago. What illusions! At the time there was still an attorney general in Munich, who dared to call a brown shirt murder a murder, and who openly took action against the killer in brown uniform because of murder. Attorney General Wintersberger filed this action and asked for the arrest of Kantschuster, the S. S. man who shot and killed our compatriot in the faith, Dr. Alfred Strauss, in May 1933 in Dachau. The interrogation of the killer disclosed the picture of an arrogant, stupid, submissive tool of the Nazis. I can still see him at the interrogation....

(We hear the voice of the Stormtrooper)

Stormtrooper: No! Let me tell you how it happened. I'd been ordered to take out prisoner Strauss. I didn't care who he was: a lawyer, whatever ... he's a Jew, and I had to act, eh, ... accordingly. Just as we were outside of the camp, I, eh ... I had to take a leak.... The prisoner then tried to take advantage of this moment ... to escape ... so, I followed orders. I fired ... and the Jew fell.

Leo Baeck: No word of regret, no sign of remorse … the dead did not count.…

Neumeyer: That is the reality.

IV

Speaker: Rabbi Baeck was only taken after almost the entire remaining Jewish community of Berlin had been deported. He was sent to the concentration camp at Theresienstadt. His inmate number was 187,894. Daily, he had to cart the garbage of the entire camp to a dumpsite outside. He was assisted by a Jewish professor of philosophy from Holland, who helped him pull the cart with its heavy, stinking containers. They called themselves "the team"; the rabbi on the right, and Professor Bousemaa on the left. On the way they would discuss the latest pages of the manuscript, which the rabbi wanted to complete while in the camp. Theresienstadt was not as much of a hellhole as the other concentration camps; it operated as a preliminary passage to Hell. Rabbi Baeck, now 70 years old, was hungry, tired and not used to hard, physical labor. Yet all he spoke about was the secret and the paradox of Jewish thought. According to the Common Era, it was now 1943.

Leo Baeck: I mean the tension between the God of the distance, the God of the mysterious, of the irrational, and the God who is known to us, the God who is close. In the tension between the Creator and the created, the individuality of Judaism is best expressed. The tension between the God who is far and the God who is near, between transcendence and imminence, is the expression of ethic tension in human nature. These two qualities of God, distance and closeness, are always shown next to each other.

Bousemaa: Phew! You take a little rest now. What a strong team we are.

Leo Baeck:	Nothing in the world is empty and without sacredness. I have to think of the teachings of the Chasidim just here. There is something holy in everything, waiting for redemption. It, therefore, is a commandment for us to search for the holy in the mundane.
Stormtrooper:	Hey, you there. What are you lazy Jews up to? Stop yakking and get back to work. This is no coffee-klatch. (coming closer) Wait a minute, you … with the beard … aren't you Rabbi Baeck, the chief kike?
Leo Baeck:	I am Leo Baeck.
Stormtrooper:	The commandant is looking for you. He's got a nice, cushy job for you, you old fart. You're to be put in charge of carrying out our orders; you will make the selecting list of the sick and weak … who'll move on. Be at his office this afternoon … get it?!
Leo Baeck:	Yes, I understand.
Stormtrooper:	Yes <u>Sir</u>, I understand! You shithead…. Who's your buddy, huh? Yet another rabbi?
Bousemaa:	I am a professor of philosophy, from Holland.
Stormtrooper:	Some team!
Speaker:	The stormtrooper leaves.
Bousemaa:	Ah, hard not to curse him.
Leo Baeck:	Where were we … Our people?…
Bousemaa:	(shaking head) You know, you amaze me. You hardly get you breath back and your thoughts are back with your papers.

V

Speaker:	It is now 1944, the year 5704 of the Jewish calendar. Week after week, more and more people are shipped out of Theresienstadt. Everyone knows where they are going. Rabbi Baeck too knows it. They will be gassed. Because they are Jews, no other reason. Human brains

invented the gas chambers. Human beings of people who had been their neighbors. Rabbi Baeck becomes a Zaddik jessod olam, a pillar that supports the world. His word counts. It counts for all those who love him. It counts for those who must die. Several hundred a week. Rabbi Baeck is forbidden to continue his lectures to his community of Jews—lectures on themes of his book that dealt with Jewish existence—yet he somehow always finds ways to get around this order. At night, he gathered his comrades in the attic of the barrack and talked to them. No one betrayed him.

Leo Baeck: Moses asked, "Who is God?" or, as expressed in the old language, what is God's name. The answer, the revelation, says that God is the Existing One, the I as Being, and the Being as the I, that God, the eternal "I Am," is this eternal unity of I and being.

First Voice: Rabbi, there is not time to talk.

    We need your help. It is important.

Leo Baeck: What happened?

Second Voice: For tomorrow morning they plan a double transport. They sent us the list. We should choose—with you, Rabbi.

Leo Baeck: And if I refuse?

Second Voice: You cannot refuse ... and let us alone take the responsibility.

Leo Baeck: But you said twice as many this time?...

First Voice: That means we also have to choose among the strong ones?...

Leo Baeck: And if I refuse? I don't mean that I want to refuse because I am afraid. It will only be a question of time ... and they will ask for me ... you know that.

Second Voice: Me too ... I am reconciled....

First Voice:	Me too. Only the heart cries out, cries for survival. The intelligence no longer.
Leo Baeck:	And if I refuse?
First Voice:	That would make everything more difficult. They would herd numbers together ... but through you, we remain human.
Second Voice:	And also Jews.
Michael:	Rabbi, I need to talk to you.
Leo Baeck:	I now have less time than no time.
Michael:	It has to be now.
Leo Baeck:	Who are you, my boy?
Michael:	I'm Michael, I'm 18, but they are not after me. I know, Rabbi, why they called you. I beg you, select me. Select me before all others....
Leo Baeck:	Do you have a father, an uncle, whose place you want to take?
Michael:	My parents and all relatives have left already....
Leo Baeck:	And why do you come to me, Michael?
Michael:	Exchange me for someone you love. I want to please you, Rabbi.
Leo Baeck:	Michael ... "One who resembles God?" That's the name you carry. Who resembles God?
Michael:	I always remember my name....
Leo Baeck:	I wish that you just stay alive ... here ... with me ... even if it is only a short time ... that also takes courage, Michael.
Michael:	Living, is that possible here? How is that possible?
Leo Baeck:	Never to give in. Never to capitulate before the dirt. Not to resign in the face of meanness. Not to become a mere number, and also to preserve self-respect....

(fade out)

VI

Speaker:	The month of Nissan, of the year 5705 of the Jewish calendar, April 1945, Common Era. Rabbi Baeck was separated from the other inmates and put in solitary confinement, but was allowed to continue his writing. He wrote about Moses, the man with the Egyptian name and the Jewish soul.
Leo Baeck:	This man and these people are one. The five books which are named after him closed with the words "Moses" and "Israel"—"Moses before the eyes of all Israel." He was the great designer of the people. His soul entered the soul of the people. He understood himself in this people, and this nation learned to understand itself in him. He created this nation for the mission?…
Speaker:	At this moment, the camp commandant, the infamous Adolf Eichmann, entered the cell.
Leo Baeck:	Prisoner 187,894 … Leo Baeck.
Eichmann:	Your full name.
Leo Baeck:	Leo Israel Baeck.
Eichmann:	(checking his papers) Baeck … I thought you'd died long ago.
Leo Baeck:	You seem to predict a future event.
Eichmann:	(not paying attention, studying his list) According to the list, Rabbi Baeck was shipped out long ago—I thought this case was closed. Was there another Rabbi Beck?
Leo Baeck:	He spelled his name with an e, not ae, as I do.
Eichmann:	All right! You have two days. In the morning … Mr. Baeck.
Leo Baeck:	I know. I would like to finish a few things.

Eichmann:	Finish. You have time to do it.
Leo Baeck:	Would you let Michael, my young assistant ... could he be with me once more?
Eichmann:	So ordered. We are not subhuman, you know.
Speaker:	Commandant Adolf Eichmann leaves and, for two days, Rabbi Baeck is reunited with Michael.
Leo Baeck:	(to himself) There is one thing, in all its variations, that basically is one which God brought out in the Jewish people. God gave them the will for the unconditional, the courage to accept the invisible, Ruling One. This spirit of decision and willingness comes from God.
Michael:	(entering) Rabbi Baeck? It is I, Michael....
Leo Baeck:	Who is like God?
Michael:	I am allowed to be with you for three minutes ... no longer.
Leo Baeck:	Now I know, Michael, why they saved me so long. They haven't saved me at all. In Munich they read another name for mine.
Michael:	I want to go with you.
Leo Baeck:	Michael, don't talk like that. We became friends, and I am giving you the little that I wish to see in the hands of a friend. Here: the wedding rings of my wife and mine, a few farewell letters, and the pages of a book which I was unable to finish completely. And now, I am waiting for what is coming.
Michael:	Rabbi, why shouldn't I go with you? How long am I allowed to keep the rings, the letters, and the book?...
Leo Baeck:	Don't ask, Michael. Do what I ask of you. And when they also call you to get ready for the trip, then turn over rings, letters, and the book ... again to a friend ... if you are able to do it....
Michael:	And if I cannot do it?

Leo Baeck:	Before the martyrdom of death is the martyrdom of life; before the courage of death, the courage to live, which many times is more difficult.

VII

(Russian Music)	
Speaker:	Two days later, in the morning—the very morning upon which Leo Baeck was to go to his death—a liberating Russian army reached the camp Theresienstadt and opened the gates. They were free. Rabbi Baeck implored the Jews not to seek revenge on their oppressors.
Leo Baeck:	We stand before our God. With the same strengths with which we confess our sins on the day of atonement, the sins of the individual and the whole. We say it with a feeling of disgust, that we see under our feet the lie which turned against our religion and its testimony. We pledge ourselves to our faith and our future. We stand before our God. We build on the Holy One. In God our history, our waiting under all changes, our determination under all circumstances have their truth and honor. Our history is a history of spiritual greatness, spiritual dignity. Let us not look back, not in hate and anger, upon our tormentors. Let us keep away from hate and revenge, because hate and revenge lower those who practice them.
Speaker:	At this moment, a Russian Colonel approached.
Leo Baeck:	Let us turn in gratefulness to our Russian liberators. (applause)
Russian Colonel:	Da—thank you yes. You have decided? What shall happen to this Nazi pig, your camp commandant?
Leo Baeck:	I ask to have him put before a court. Protect him ... for justice.
Russian Colonel:	You have the power over him?...

Leo Baeck:	No, it is my duty to ask and to pray that justice be done.
Russian Colonel:	Rabbi, also, an American plane has landed outside.
Leo Baeck:	Are they coming in?
Russian Colonel:	… American airplane only take Rabbi Baeck … that is you … yes?
Leo Baeck:	Yes, but the others?…
Russian Colonel:	They can only take you; the Rabbi, they said.
Leo Baeck:	I remain until the last Jew leaves the camp. I stay until then.
Russian Colonel:	Please, you say this to Americans yourselves.
Leo Baeck:	Yes, yes, I will tell them and give them thanks.
Russian Colonel:	And, what about this Nazi … your camp commandant?
Leo Baeck:	Punishment … according to law.
Russian Colonel:	You're a good man, Rabbi … too good. Germans, they have desecrated Russia … like to you Jews; millions of Russians died, like you Jews. "Justice for them?" Nyet! Remember, we Russians saved your lives.
Leo Baeck:	I am grateful to you from the bottom of my heart.
Russian Colonel:	Da, da. You want to fly in the plane … yes or no?
Leo Baeck:	The sick, at least some of them should go out on this plane. Like Michael, my young friend … he has high fever. Dysentery. He should go first.
Russian Colonel:	Rabbi, it is getting late. You <u>must</u> go, yes? Ah but first talk with your people here. I think they are getting restless.
Leo Baeck:	My friends, my family. We stand before our God. Whose commandment, which we obey, gives us strength. We follow God, and we stand erect before the world. We serve God, and we remain firm during all the changes in history. Humbly we trust God, and our

course lies clearly before us, we see our futures. Our prayer, our confidence, our confession is that of all Jews on earth. We look at each other and we know, and we look up to our God, and we know about what which lasts. Sorrow and pain fill us. We want to express in silence, through moments of silence before our GOD, that which fills our souls. This silent service will be more impressive than words can express....

(fade out)

VIII

Speaker:

In the years that followed, Leo Baeck lived in London. Although he considered the history of Jews in Germany as finished, he did not retire, feeling that his faith ordered him to work on behalf of his fellow believers. It forced him to continue to teach according to the books of the Torah. He had finished the book, <u>This People Israel</u>, on which he had worked in the concentration camp, and he now worked on a second volume. One day, he received a letter from Germany. They would be happy to welcome him at a convention.

Leo Baeck:

I won't forget what they did to us as a people. We should not forget in the name of the victims. But I'll not refuse, if they want to make a new beginning. I have many friends among the Germans. It was not their fault that they could not prevent this misfortune. They had to experience the demise of the empire.... In the beginning I want to go to the German Jews. There are new Jewish communities; the survivors are getting together. There are those who returned. The German-Jewish symbiosis was always my pet idea. We also should not forget; there was a common martyrdom, of Jews, pious Christians, and many, many others. They, like us, were in those camps, despised and mocked. And for Germany? What can we hope for Germany? Hitler's revolution was a revolution of the German Philistines, not that of the German worker. The Philistines elected this monster ... these people without a tomorrow, who would be justified through their success, because they believed to have their judgment because they had success. This _man_ of satisfaction and without problem, this _man_ without a tomorrow, joined the person without a past, this upstart.... I want to tell them of Moses ben Maimon, of Maimonides. The Jewish Orient and the Jewish West considered themselves as one through him. Many great Germans of past centuries honored him. Albertus Magnus, Nikolaus von Cues, Meister Eckhardt, Leibnitz ... I have to tell them again. _Why_? Out of gratefulness; we are a grateful people. Those who have helped us are never forgotten, their memory remains. Their name is remembered from generation to generation, as a permanent blessing. How often are there days when we are filled with sorrow and pain. But we can find solace, if we have people in our midst whom we can gratefully remember. Those who are—kind, just and unselfish—who give an example of what we should be. Therein lies, profoundly, a blessed certainty, a guarantee for our future....

(fade out)

Speaker: Rabbi Leo Baeck died at the age of 83 in London, on November 2, 1956. That was the 28th day of the month Cheschwan of the year 5717 of the Jewish Calendar. The German President, Theodor Heuss, who knew and respected Rabbi Baeck, wrote at that time, "I believe that Rabbi Baeck saw his fate and his task with understanding, strength, and love, without fanfare; he lived a life of trial filled with happiness and sorrow that should become a symbol. Nobody should think of mourning. Everyone who knew him will feel the need to thank him.

I want to be able to express how beautiful, how right, indeed how necessary, I consider it to present this picture of his character to the world.

978-0-595-42426-9
0-595-42426-0

Lightning Source UK Ltd.
Milton Keynes UK
27 April 2010

153442UK00001B/181/A